THE 21 DAY DOORWAY ACROSS THE VEIL

MARY BERTUN

Copyright © 2020 by Mary Bertun

All rights reserved. This book or any portion thereof may not be reproduced or used in any manner whatsoever without the express written permission of the publisher except for the use of brief quotations in a book review.

Printed in the United States of America

First Printing, 2020

ISBN 978-1-7346586-0-6 Paperback

ISBN 978-1-7346586-2-0 Hardcover

Faith in Angels

314 Marston Avenue

Madison, Wisconsin 53703

https://faithinangels.academy/

I dedicate this journal with the warmest love to my wonderful son Chas Bertun, a Marine who left this earth in 2012. In truth, Chas is my coauthor.

PREFACE

For me, writing has become an act of love.

Once I would have said I knew all about love, but in reality I knew nothing. After my son's transition it did not take me long to learn about the unbreakable link between love and humility. I was humbled by the wisdom Spirit offered and blown away to hear my son's voice.

Writing down the words, every day, is the way I show my gratitude and love.

Throughout the book I will offer you structure to practice listening and writing down the words from loved ones in spirit. As you start using these techniques, you'll open your awareness and listen with your heart rather than your head. Your realizations and awakenings will happen not because of my words, but because of your experiences as you act on these practices.

What emerges will be your own, as gifted by those you love in heaven.

I would like to thank my truly awesome Helping Parents Heal co-leader Tava Wilson, who edited my workbook draft. We witnessed an amazing sign from Tava's daughter Christina during this editing work. The story is Tava's to share, but it involves inexplicable changes in phone information and photos. This was Christina's way of sending a message of love to a family member.

Seeing such a miracle leads me to believe we are on the right path.

Thanks also go to all those who volunteered to participate in a January 2020 class and further refine this workbook. Your connections are stunning.

<u>Class Participants</u>

Rhonda and Reece Andrews

Donna and Peter Scott Bullwinkel

Patti Dever and Samantha Scott

Shannon and Dominque Jasmine (aka Pickle) Hache

Brenda and Trevin Horn

Mary Johnson and Austin Johnson-Voice

Kathy Fitzgibbons MacMannis and Aiden and Conor MacMannis

Claire and Pamela Martin

Alicia Moag-Stahlberg and Kristen Marie (aka Kiki) Stahlberg

Cathie and Christopher Westdyk

Tava Wilson and Christina Tourant

INTRODUCTION

Communication with your loved one in spirit begins by changing the things you do daily. You are finding that person where they are now, and that takes a certain path with specific skills.

That you are here, reading and writing in a journal that guides you as you communicate across the veil, is big step. Give yourself some well-deserved credit and know that you are among friends.

There are challenges as you listen to a voice from heaven and this workbook will support you as you question and discover answers. Here's the real secret. Your internal journey is unique. You will tackle changes in your daily routine and develop yourself spiritually once you commit to this path.

The death of a loved one is never wanted. This death leaves a gaping hole in your heart. When I lost my 19-year-old son Chas in 2012, my heart broke in so many pieces, I did not know how I was ever going to put all those pieces back together.

You too desperately miss your loved one who has crossed over. You miss their presence, their voice, their smiles, their hugs, and 1001 things you feel you will never have again until the day you join that loved one in heaven. All of us hunger for that missing relationship. What do we do with the longing?

Quickly we learn that pleading for the loved one's return, does not translate into experiencing that loved one beside us. I am blessed to be an affiliate leader for Helping Parents Heal (https://www.helpingparentsheal.org/). We talk regularly at our meetings about "how" to experience the presence of our child in heaven. We can develop our relationship with our children different from and BEYOND what we had with them while they breathed here on earth.

There are some practical steps to take when communicating with your loved one in spirit. The focus of this workbook is on how to listen and then write down what you hear. These steps have awakened me to the presence of my son Chas in my life on earth.

Many people have used other methods of making contact – use of mediums, cards or rune stone readings, use of a pendulum, or focusing on signs/synchronicities observed. I say use what works for you because there are amazing stories of success with such approaches.

But in this workbook, we're looking at you sharing a real conversation with your loved one in spirit. Any form of true communication requires both a sender and a receiver. In other words, just speaking out or wishing without listening for the response, is not communication.

Desire, combined with asking divine sources for help, most often leads to success. Here we aim to show you the steps for that direct, desired conversation and detail how to reach out for assistance.

If you plan to stretch your heart to a point of wide-open, to show more faith in the power of love to restore you, than in the power of fear to destroy you – well then, this workbook is for you!

How to Use This Workbook

We hope by writing down your experiences, you'll have the success that inspires you to continue the spiritual journey after the end of the 21 days. Writing focuses your brain on the physical process. This allows your spirit to reach out to your loved one in heaven without hindrance.

As you journal, you'll become more aware of the presence of your loved one. If you dedicate yourself to this effort, listening and writing down the words you hear, it is my hope that this will transform your life, as it has mine.

How do you recognize your loved one's voice?

When a spirit in heaven speaks to you, the thoughts come spontaneously. When we ourselves are thinking, our mind moves from one idea to the next. When you receive a thought from those in spirit, it will seem like the words just dropped into your mind. At times this happens so rapidly, you realize you could not have created the thought.

When you want to hear from a specific loved one in heaven, you will make that intention crystal clear as part of the steps you follow. Bear in mind that the spirit who steps forward to communicate is who we need to hear from in that moment. If that spirit is not your specified loved one – where are they? Right beside the spirit who is speaking – your loved one has never left you and will not miss this opportunity to converse.

Often the words you hear from heaven will be light and healing. The flow of information is easily cut off by your will or thoughts which have you jumping to another idea. To stay in the receptive mode, you will need a technique to bring your focus back to silence and listening. I return my focus by looking at an object on my desk and so am reminded to start listening once again. That voice from heaven? It has never left you. But statistics collected at Arthur Findlay College in England indicate that only 45% of what is being transmitted is received. That means we have to be willing to maintain our focus, when our mind starts to wander.

At times the instructions will suggest you use your heart, rather than your mind as you communicate. How do you do this? It seems like a tough concept, but it's actually a simple switch that uses your memory.

Remember the treasured, sacred moments you keep in your heart – times of joy and great love. To use your heart, rather than your mind, imagine your heart opening to display those same treasures which are yours to keep. Let these sacred memories guide the decision or action you must take. Such precious feelings, from your heart, will steer you in the right direction.

You will be guided to be in a receptive state throughout this journal. Do not review what you've written down until after your journaling session ends. Start by practicing for 10-15 minutes and later expand this to 30 minutes as you are comfortable with the process. Write either during or after your listening session.

As you recognize words from those in heaven, you are training your spiritual senses to distinguish between your own thoughts and theirs. As you are more sensitive to how your loved one in spirit is communicating with you, what was once difficult will become easy.

Steps to Use

Step 1: Find a comfortable place to write. Your back should be supported and you should be in a place that allows you to shut out the outside world. For awhile I wrote while propped up in bed. But soon I received direct requests to sit at my desk. There was great rejoicing when I made this switch, and now I understand why.

Having the right tools and equipment for the road ahead is important, as is the physical body that makes this adventure possible. Find the place that works best for you.

Step 2: Arrange a few favorite things that will be in your immediate line of vision, near your writing surface. These items should pull your focus back when your mind wants to wander. You want to prepare to enjoy this process. Some folks will light a candle, others may choose to use the essential oils of aromatherapy. Your loved one will appreciate that you are making the effort to raise your vibration and meet them part of the way. Put on your favorite music a few minutes prior to starting your practice and admire how you've set up this area. Everything else gets easier once you find the joy in this communication.

Step 3: It is important to conduct your practice with a pure heart. Tell your ego that you are placing it along with your fears, concerns, and judgements on a back shelf, just while you are practicing. It is critical to begin your practice with a prayer of protection. You may pray to any divine entity you choose. I pray to Archangel Michael, who has a well-deserved reputation as a protector and leader. I say: "Dear Archangel Michael, please surround me with protection and love, so that only words for my greater good come through as I write. I ask you Archangel Michael to silence my fears and stray thoughts so that I listen closely for those in spirit, especially."

(name) _____

Step 4: Listen. Can you truly hear what another person is saying if you let your mind wander? Give your full attention to Spirit and listening. Those in heaven always try to create a moment of awareness so you'll know they're there. Offer your thanks and gratitude to your loved one in spirit. Be fully present by stating silently or out loud, "I am always here for you!" Allow happiness to well up inside, because you're about to hear from heaven. Don't rush this or try to analyze it, because if you do – it's gone. Feel with your heart and embrace any sounds you hear. This is the beginning of your communication.

Step 5: Write. As words, phrases, sounds, song comes to you, simply record this on paper. This starts the discussion between you and a loved one in spirit. You are meant to discern that loved one's presence in your life and in your heart.

Quickly write what comes to you, without judging. At first you may use the prompts or questions in the workbook to speak out to those in heaven. But do not dwell on these words, just move into attentive listening. Write either during or after you listen. This is your conversation, and once started the words will flow.

There's all the time in the world to later review what you've written down.

Some Tips

1. Build the foundation of awareness. Have patience and perseverance, rather than rushing ahead. Find time for silence and the unseen world. You are fine tuning your receptivity and heightening your senses. Practice 5-10 minutes each day until you are ready to lengthen the time you spend.

2. Your body may react to the changes in energy as you begin to hear spirit – tears or a fast beating heart are commonly reported. If this is concerning to you, say to yourself "This is merely a response to a change in energy " Then focus on your breathing to restore balance.

3. Be aware of how your own thoughts formulate – what clearly comes from your own brain. This will help you discern or distinguish what is <u>not</u> from your mind.

4. Listening to music or high vibrational sounds may ease

your readiness for listening to spirit. When you practice, you are touching your soul's memory banks and bringing the conscious and unconscious together. Music might well be an effective tool.

Considerations

Beyond asking for your loved one to communicate, how do you open your broken heart rather than your mind?

Remember, it is your *mind's job* to remind you constantly about the source of your pain. If something causes us pain, like a hot stove, our mind's job is to remind us to never touch that hot stove again, to make sure we remember how painful it was the first time.

For that reason, the mind causes us to obsess about the source of our pain, our loved one's transition to heaven, and the fact that they are no longer physically present on earth. Guilt, anger, anguish, and self-doubt are all strategies our mind is willing to employ. The mind can be quite the deceiver, but hey, it's only doing its job.

Logic and analytic thought dominate our culture. Being rational is not a bad thing. But how do you listen to your heart even as your mind disagrees? Make no mistake, when we try to communicate with our loved one in heaven, we must listen with the heart, not the mind.

You are learning a new language here and laying down a new foundation. That's not easy work, but it is so so worth the effort. As we begin journaling, we will start to build the practice of listening with our heart rather than our mind. And we'll do that by reflecting on our feelings as we face life's choices. Please use the technique listed on Page x and recall the sacred moments you hold close in your heart.

Be patient with the practice of learning to listen to your heart. It takes far more time than just a few days spent with your journal. But if you're like me, and you truly understand the need for doing this work, one day it will just all click into place. You'll find yourself listening with your beautiful heart in most situations.

Your loved one in heaven will applaud your efforts to grow and listen with your heart. That soul is growing as well and wants to see you reuniting with your higher self. In doing this work, you are not letting go of your loved one, you are deepening the relationship.

Let's get started.

WEEK 1
AWAKEN YOUR HEART

DAY 1

No spiritual master who ever walked the earth has anything on you. You're the complete package, the real deal. You just don't remember it yet.

       Carrie Triffet, <u>The Enlightenment Project</u>

Do I feel my decision to use this workbook and listen for my loved one in spirit, in my brain or in my heart?

Has my loved one reached out to me in other ways - synchronicities, signs, etc.?

Find your place of silence and calm. Write down any thoughts, feelings or impressions you have at this moment.

DAY 2

Your guardian angel never, ever stops communicating with you. I feel that at times they should be frustrated with us but they seem to have endless patience and they never ever give up on us.

Lorna Byrne, <u>Angels In My Hair</u>

YOU ARE USED to being strong for others. Who do your turn to when you need help with understanding your higher self?

You were perfectly made and chosen for this life on earth. How do you think your guardian angel sees you?

For the answer to this question, find a photo of yourself when you were 2-5 years old. Place the photo in a location where you will see it several times a day, maybe as the wallpaper on your cell phone.

Can you treat yourself as the beautiful soul the angels see?

Find your place of quiet and record your notes after considering the questions above.

DAY 3

Let me share a personal story, one that took place as I was trying to connect with my son Chas in the early days of my grief journey. I'm still not sure who answered my question, I only know it was not my son.

I asked "What are you learning now in heaven?"

The answer came so swiftly I didn't have time to think it up. But I knew this came from someone other than Chas, and that the message was for me.

"This is like going over a narrow rope stretched across a deep ravine. You can run across it swiftly, increasing the risk of falling or crashing on the other side. Or you can move more slowly, balancing with each step you take. If you choose the latter, I will be by your side helping you balance each step. Your choice."

How do you want to learn the lessons of this lifetime - alone or relying on divine guidance?

If you are willing to accept guidance, does it matter who in heaven provides that help?

After you have thought about these questions, ask for divine assistance with the following exercise and record your results.

Exercise for Deepening Awareness

When you are in a group of people, focus on and isolate one voice. This strengthens your awareness of the singular and so, the sound of a spirit voice amongst all the other sounds you may hear.

DAY 4

In <u>A Course in Miracles,</u> there is that line "many are called, but few are chosen". This means that everyone is called but few care to listen.

We are all being called at every moment. We are being called to express our better selves and rise to the occasions in life. To be forgiving and compassionate, to choose love instead of fear, to not sink into the mire of our patterns, woundedness, and victimization.

Marianne Williamson, Teaching the Teachers video course

How do you **feel about asking your Guardian Angel or other divine source for help in setting aside fears, anger, patterns, and deep sorrows?**

Let your heart, rather than your logic, guide your answer to this question. Write your notes in your journal.

DAY 5

Five years after my son Chas transitioned, I went to a retreat where we discussed <u>A Course in Miracles.</u> One evening we attended a singing bowls concert. In a room lit only by candles, I sat off in one corner. As the first sounds rose up, the shadow of my son darted into the corner behind me. Chas rested a hand on my shoulder and whispered "Here, Mom" in my ear.

I thought it a good thing the room was dark because tears began to stream down my face. I was further amazed to notice shadow after shadow, maybe a dozen or more, darting into the same small corner. I was shown that these were Chas's friends in spirit. They were there not only to hear the beautiful music, but also to support Chas's effort to be with me.

As you might imagine, the joy and happiness stayed with me for days.

TODAY WE BEGIN **our practice of deep listening. First you're setting up your quiet place. Keep this workbook or another type of journal in the immediate area, to jot down notes.**

Take a few minutes to find a clearing in the dense forest of your

life, a place to experience silence and peace. Let go of worries, plans, sorrow and anything else that takes your attention. Say a brief prayer of protection and ask your Guardian Angel to help you to be here, fully present. Invite a smile to your face as you settle into a restful mode. Ask your Angels or Guides if they'd like you to practice with your eyes open or closed. Follow the first direction that pops into mind.

Practice your mindfulness for no more than 10-12 minutes. When you start where you are, be prepared to feel that familiar tug to something in your environment or your own thoughts. But you will begin to hear an inner voice more clearly as you focus on being present, in this moment. If your mind wanders, bring it gently and kindly back. Do this by focusing on your breath.

In a place of calm and peace, say, "I am here for you, beloved. I am happy you are here!"

Continue to focus on staying present and listening for any sound or voice that may place a word, phrase or song in your mind. After your practice has ended, write down notes on anything you felt, heard, or saw. Or write during your session, whatever approach works best for you.

DAY 6

Expect An Answer

As drought continued for what seemed an eternity, a small community of farmers was in a quandary as to what to do. Rain was important to keep their crops healthy and sustain the way of life of the townspeople.

As the problem became more acute, a local pastor called a prayer meeting to ask for rain.

Many people arrived. The pastor greeted most of them as they filed in. As he walked to the front of the church to officially begin the meeting he noticed most people were chatting across the aisles and socializing with friends. When he reached the front his thoughts were on quieting the attendees and starting the meeting.

His eyes scanned the crowd as he asked for quiet. He noticed an eleven year-old girl sitting quietly in the front row.

Her face was beaming with excitement!

Next to her, poised and ready for use, was a bright red umbrella. The little girl's beauty and innocence made the pastor smile as he realized how much faith she possessed.

No one else in the congregation had brought an umbrella.

All came to pray for rain, but the little girl had come expecting someone from heaven to answer.

Author unknown and greatly appreciated

FIND YOUR PLACE of quiet. Keep this workbook or another type of journal in the immediate area, to jot down notes. If you want to light a candle or use music to lift your spirit, do so.

Go to that place to where you experience silence and peace. Let go of worries, plans, sorrow and anything else that takes your attention. Say a brief prayer of protection and ask your Guardian Angel to help you to be here, fully present. Invite a smile to your face as you settle into a restful mode. Again, ask your Angels or Guides if they'd like you to practice with your eyes open or closed. Follow the first direction that pops into mind.

Practice your mindfulness for no more than 10-12 minutes. If your mind wanders, bring it gently and kindly back. Do this by focusing on your breath. One by one, shut the doors of your senses, leaving only your sense of hearing open.

In a place of calm and peace, say, "I am here for you, beloved. I am happy you are here!"

Continue to focus on staying present and listening for any sound or voice that may place a word, phrase or song in your mind. After a minute has passed, say "I am here, ready to hear anything you might tell me."

During or after your practice has ended, write down notes on anything you felt, heard, or saw.

11/4/20

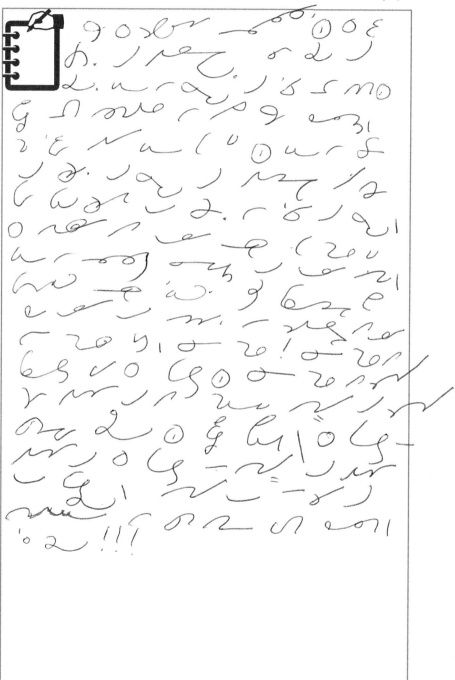

DAY 7

In the early months after my son transitioned, gratitude was perhaps the furthest thing from my mind. But I learned an important lesson one day that placed gratitude as something I wanted most in my life.

We replaced a bench in the corner of the park across from our house, with a memorial plaque that welcomes all who sit there. I started placing flowers in a vase to one side of the bench and often included a note to share Chas memories with others.

The summer after my son's passing, one man occupied the bench for several weeks. He sat there for hours at a time, head buried in his hands, sometimes rocking back and forth. At times the man slept on the bench.

I didn't want to intrude, but I began to worry how I might refresh the flowers. Early one Saturday the bench appeared empty, so I hurried over with a note and some fresh flowers. I was stunned by the sight that met my eyes. A collection of items was arranged around the previous week's flowers. These things had the look of stuff collected in the park – some grubby beads, mismatched single earrings, a frayed friendship bracelet and parts of a necklace.

What was this junk doing there? It took a few seconds before I realized that the man who had occupied the bench had left this collection as either a tribute or a thank you.

Care had been taken arranging the jewelry. It was a message of such incredible sweetness, I found it hard to breathe. So much had been offered by one who had so little.

FIND YOUR PLACE of calm and silence. Take a comfortable position and try to clear your mind of the day's concerns. Look over the past week and make note of those times when you felt Spirit or your loved one in heaven was nudging you toward something in your life. How did you feel during those times you were trying to respond to that nudge? Did someone in heaven feel present to you at that moment? Note the details in the space provided.

Return to your place of silence and peace. Say a brief prayer of protection and ask your Guardian Angel to help you to be here, fully present. Let those in Spirit know you feel gratitude for the guidance you received this past week. Invite a smile to your face as you settle into a restful mode.

Practice your mindfulness for no more than 15-20 minutes. If your mind wanders, bring it gently and kindly back. Do this by focusing on your breath. One by one, shut the doors of your senses, leaving only your sense of hearing open.

In a place of calm and peace, say, "I am here for you, beloved. I am happy you are here!"

Continue to focus on staying present and listening for any sound or voice that may place a word, phrase or song in your mind. During or after your session, note what occurred in your journal.

WEEK 2
LISTENING IN DEEP SILENCE

DAY 8

You can't help but feel gratitude in heaven, but I should have spent more time cultivating it on earth. Gratitude puts you in the frame of mind where much is possible. It is the gateway to joy.

Quote by Chas Bertun

FIND YOUR PLACE of calm and silence. Take a comfortable position and try to clear your mind of the day's concerns. Think of your loved one in heaven and your gratitude for having that precious person in your life.

Return to your place of silence and peace. Say a brief prayer of protection and ask your Guardian Angel to help you to be here, fully present. Welcome in those in Spirit (Angels or Guides) and thank them for ministering to you this moment. What would you most like to hear those in spirit say? Smile as you settle into a restful mode.

Practice for no more than 15-20 minutes. If your mind wanders, bring it gently and kindly back. You are listening for the voice of those in Spirit.

In a place of calm and peace, say, "I am here for you, beloved. I am grateful you are here!"

Continue to focus on staying present and listening for any sound or voice that may place a word, phrase or song in your mind. During or after your session write your notes in your journal.

DAY 9

Listen well. Not all obstacles lead you in the wrong direction.

Quote by a Guardian Angel Aiden

WE ARE USING mindfulness to connect with our loved ones in Spirit because that is where they are, in the here and now, not in our memories of the past.

To do this you are meeting whatever is in your heart and mind with acceptance, instead of avoidance or resistance. Rather than diving into or dwelling on your thoughts, you are bringing your attention back to the here and now.

There are two ways to do this. The first, focusing on your breath is helpful if your mind is busy and active. As the great Thich Nhat Hanh has stated, "Joy and happiness are possible with your in-breath and your out-breath."

But if your mind is calm and settled, use the second method of unfocused awareness. With this method your mind is like a wide-open sky- anything can pass through it, everything can come and go like the clouds.

With this second method, you can retain receptive awareness and listen.

Return to your place of silence and quiet. Say a brief prayer of protection and ask your Guardian Angel to help you to be here, fully present. Add in your thoughts of gratitude for the team in spirit that assists you. Smile as you settle into peace.

Let your loved ones in spirit know that you are fully present and available to hear whatever may be shared. Once you know your mind is calm, use your awareness as a wide-open sky. As the clouds of thoughts, concerns , and worries drift away, listen to the sound of spirit that only you can hear.

Write down any details of your experience in your journal, anything you hear, feel or see.

DAY 10

In grief, we often entangle the past, the present, and future. We need to come into the present moment so we're getting our meaning from the now, not the then.

David Kessler, <u>Finding Meaning the Sixth Stage of Grief</u>

ONCE YOU BECOME comfortable with silence, *you can come to see it as a presence rather than an absence.*

Today marks a different phase of practice where we are sensing spiritual presence.

Find your place of silence and peace. Sit down, with pen in hand, and open the journal that will hold your notes. Say a prayer of protection and express your gratitude. Then let your mind wander aimlessly, until it comes to rest in the Presence. Listen. Write in your journal the scraps and fragments that come to you. What flows may come in the form of prayers, words spoken, a tune or a phrase.

Practice in this way for 15-20 minutes.

DAY 11

Silence is a constant source of restoration. Yet its healing power does not come cheaply. It depends on our willingness to face all that is within us, light and dark, and to heed all the inner voices that make themselves heard in silence.

The Cowley Fathers, <u>The Rule of the Society of St. John the Evangelist</u>

IT TAKES PRACTICE to learn to silence your thoughts. The important thing is to respond kindly when your thoughts intrude and using the technique that works best for you such as a focus on the breath, maintaining the open sky of awareness, or just placing thoughts on a temporary shelf while you sit and practice. Let your awareness help you discern what comes from your mind and what comes from a spiritual source.

Find your place of silence and peace. Sit down, with pen in hand, and open the journal that will hold your notes. Say a prayer of protection and express your gratitude. Then let your mind wander aimlessly, until it comes to rest in the Presence. Listen.

Write in your journal the scraps and fragments that come to you, be these prayers, words spoken, a tune or a phrase.

Practice in this way for 15-20 minutes.

DAY 12

There is only one path to Heaven. On earth, we call it Love.

Quote by Henry David Thoreau

TODAY YOU WILL start a conversation by writing to your loved one. And your loved one will be most aware not only of what you have written, but aware that you are trying to reach out. This is a new letter, even if it details things you've said before.

What do you write? Start by telling your loved one all the things you've wanted to say. Be sure to include the reasons why you are thankful this person was in your life, as well as the reasons why you love this person. If you didn't have a perfect relationship, request the forgiveness that would bring you peace.

As you close your letter, ask one or two questions of your loved one. Keep the letter near whatever journal you use to record your notes. Read your letter out loud at least once before your next practice session.

DAY 13

How They May Come to You

Sometimes we dismiss signs and messages either because we are not paying attention or we think the messages are just our thoughts. The first messages I received came through simply as thoughts. This is the way our loved ones communicate with us – telepathically. If a random thought comes into your consciousness, it could very well be someone trying to communicate with you.

Karen Noe, <u>The Rainbow Follows the Storm</u>

TODAY YOU ARE going to connect with that energy of your loved one. Just before your practice, read again the letter you wrote that person. Let your loved one know you hope to receive a sign or message in response to one of your questions. Fill your mind with the love you feel for that person.

Find your place of silence and peace. Sit down, with pen in hand, and open the journal that will hold your notes. Say a prayer of protection, then express both your gratitude and love. Listen deeply, bringing your mind back to listening if it wanders. Write in your journal the scraps and fragments that come to you, even the feelings or energies that start to surround you. Your loved one is with you. Let them connect through the feelings that have raised your vibration.

Practice in this way for 15-20 minutes.

DAY 14

I wrote my own letter to my son Chas, asking if there was anything I'd forgotten to say about connecting with our loved ones in heaven. This is his reply.

> *Remember the time you took me and my teammates to the sub shop after the soccer game? You were happy to do this – and we were hungry! The laughter and joy that day was complete. Remember the good times, the moments of pure laughter and joy. This creates the easiest time for us to step forward because you are bouncing like a balloon. We catch you on the upswing.*
>
> *Quote by Chas Bertun*

Find your place of silence and peace. Sit down, with pen in hand, and open the journal that will hold your notes. Say a prayer of protection. Give your thanks for the assistance of your team in spirit.

Then recall a particularly happy time you spent with your loved one when that soul was here on earth.

Listen. If your eyes are open, gaze with unfocused vision, always listening.

Write in your journal whatever comes to you, whatever pops into your mind. Your loved one is with you. Let them catch you on the upswing.

Practice in this way for 15-20 minutes.

WEEK 3
SENSING PRESENCE AND FINDING PEACE

DAY 15

Hindsight is so much clearer than foresight. I can look back on my life and find God's guidance in the various parts of my story, but looking ahead is more difficult. That's why it is important to look backward once in a while and listen to your life story. You may find important clues to discerning how to live every day, but you will also have important information to help guide you when you reach a major crossroad in your life.

Debra K. Farrington in <u>Hearing with Heart</u>

TODAY, TAKE A moment to review your workbook progress so far. What is the most important technique for you to use as you listen for the voice of a loved one in heaven? Do you see differences in your awareness from Day 1 to Day 14? What signs and synchronicities have you spotted outside of your daily practice?

If you have discussed your workbook activity with a friend, sit down with that person and review your answers to the questions above. In discussion, you may see that there are changes you hadn't noticed. More importantly, ask those on your team in spirit for their feedback on your progress.

Find your place of silence and peace. Sit down, with pen in hand, and open the journal that will hold your notes. Say a prayer of protection. Give your thanks for the assistance of your team in spirit.

Ask your team in spirit for their ideas on your workbook progress.

Listen. Note whatever pops into your mind in your journal, even if this makes little sense to you now.

Practice in this way for 15-20 minutes.

DAY 16

As you use the exercises in this workbook to expand your awareness and deepen your peace, you are putting a practice in place that may become a routine along the path of your spiritual journey. But some of the best messages from our loved ones in heaven are spontaneous and unexpected.

Several years after my son's transition I was in the one-step-forward, one-step-back mode. This meant for every positive step, I would add in an hour of tears thinking of the things my son could not share *with me*. I knew better, Chas witnessed every moment I experienced. But still I suffered in grief and then would retreat to the comfort of my favorite pastime, reading.

Now I had absorbed many spiritual books, but was intrigued by a friend's frequent references to Eckhart Tolle. So I checked a book of Eckhart Tolle quotes out of the library. Then the book sat with others in my bedroom until the due date approached. I thought if I just opened the book to a random page, I could figure out if it was worth the read. The book opened to this page and these notations, which were already in the book when I opened it!! :

> and within every disaster is contained the seed of grace.
>
> Throughout history, there have been women and men who, in the face of great loss, illness, imprisonment, or impending death, accepted the seemingly unacceptable and thus found "the peace that passeth all understanding."
>
> Acceptance of the unacceptable is the greatest source of grace in this world.
>
> MOM

The book contained no other highlights or marks.

—

I wish you too a wonderful, and unexpected nudge from your loved one in heaven. Your team of angels and guides know when you are ready to take a next step, and they will make such a message possible.

Find your place of silence and peace. Sit down, with pen in hand, and open the journal that will hold your notes. Say a prayer of protection. Give your thanks for the assistance of your team in spirit.

Think of the signs your loved one has given you recently and invite a smile to your face.

Listen. Note whatever pops into your mind in your journal, accepting whatever you experience.

Practice in this way for 15-20 minutes.

DAY 17

ONE DAY I insisted on listing out all the ways I could have been a better mom and prevented my son Chas from leaving this world. But his matter-of-fact response stopped me, as I considered the topic of self-compassion.

> *Well, if you don't learn it on earth, you'll have to learn it in heaven. So you may as well learn it now so you can move on to other things.*
>
> *Quote by Chas Bertun*

This guidebook is all about working on yourself and your ability to receive the blessing of communication with your loved ones in heaven. Remember to be kind to yourself and receive the love and light your special loved ones send your way.

Find your place of silence and peace. Sit down, with pen in hand, and open the journal that will hold your notes. Say a prayer of protection. Give your thanks for the assistance of your team in spirit.

Invite a smile to your face. Let your loved one know you are present for them. Ask them to connect with you and speak with you.

Listen. Note whatever happens, whatever pops into your mind, in your journal.

Practice in this way for 20-30 minutes.

DAY 18

When the mind is calm, how quickly, how smoothly, how beautifully you will perceive everything.

Quote by Paramahansa Yogananda

FINDING PEACE IS the most important step in this process. Once you are able to tap into your inner peace, you can re-create this state several times throughout your day. Each moment will be just as it is, and you will be able meet it with acceptance and kindness.

Grief and sorrow block the ability to feel peace. If these emotions are often part of your day, try to set them aside before you practice. Over time you will notice how your state of mind greatly influences your ability to reach inner peace.

Work on finding inner peace and practice this as often as you can. This is key to hearing your loved ones in spirit. Feeling peace is also a great way to begin and end each day.

Find your place of silence and peace. Sit down, with pen in hand, and open the journal that will hold your notes. Say a

prayer of protection. Give your thanks for the assistance of your team in spirit.

Invite a smile to your face. Let your mind focus on each part of your body, relaxing your muscles. When you are completely at peace, let your loved one know you are present and available.

Listen. Note whatever happens, whatever impression or thought pops into your mind. Write down everything you feel and hear in your journal.

Practice in this way for 20-30 minutes.

DAY 19

Lose all worries about the success or failure of your practice. Increasing your awareness is all that matters. Listen and notice signs of presence. You may feel a shift in energy, inside or outside of yourself. If you hear a hum or background noise in your mind, pay attention to this and be aware of increases or decreases in that noise. Do not discount clues on the presence of others from heaven. Trust your intuition as you observe these signs.

Find your place of silence and peace. Sit down, with pen in hand, and open the journal that will hold your notes. Say a prayer of protection and express your gratitude. Then let your mind wander aimlessly, until it comes to rest in the Presence.

Listen. Write in your journal the scraps and fragments that come to you, be these sounds, words spoken, a tune or a phrase, or a hum of energy.

Practice in this way for 20-30 minutes.

DAY 20

Today, like every other day, we wake up empty
and frightened. Don't open the door to the study
and begin reading. Take down the dulcimer.

Let the beauty we love be what we do.
There are hundreds of ways to kneel and kiss the ground.

Quote by Jelalludin Rumi

THE LORD GIVES everyone different gifts. Each way or method of connecting to those in spirit takes effort and consistent practice.

If you have faithfully followed the steps outlined in this workbook, you have expanded your awareness quite a bit. Know there are always different possibilities presented to you, so you can learn your lessons on earth.

As you've been doing your practice of listening, have you felt joyful or peaceful or energized or excited? If so, these practices are aligning with your gifts. If not, keep exploring other ways to connect

– in dreams, though a medium, a pendulum, or even a different type of meditation. You will feel the shift in energy when you are using the method that's right for you. And you'll receive your loved one's communication as a quick message meant just for you.

Find your place of silence and peace. Sit down, with pen in hand, and open the journal that will hold your notes. Say a prayer of protection. Give your thanks for the assistance of your team in spirit.

Invite a smile to your face. When you are completely at peace, let your loved one know you are present and available. Ask if they have a message to give you.

Listen. Note whatever happens, whatever impression or thought pops into your mind. Write down everything you feel and hear in your journal.

Practice in this way for 20-30 minutes.

DAY 21

The one vital quality which they (the saints of old) had in common was spiritual receptivity. Something in them was open to heaven, something which urged them Godward.

Without attempting anything like a profound analysis, I shall say simply that they had spiritual awareness, and that they went on to cultivate it until it became the biggest thing in their lives.

They differed from the average person in that when they felt the inward longing, they did something about it. They acquired the lifelong habit of spiritual response.

A. W. Tozer, <u>The Pursuit of God</u>

WHEN YOU LOVE deeply, your brain clings to the activities society tells us are the proper way to remember someone who has transitioned to heaven. Gently remove these expectations from your mind.

By committing to inner peace and listening for the voice of your loved one in heaven, you commit to finding that loved one where they are now. And you are starting a real conversation.

Keep the practices that work for you. Keep your courage and determination as you let in the light.

Find your place of silence and peace. Sit down, with pen in hand, and open the journal that will hold your notes. Say a prayer of protection. Give your thanks for the assistance of your team in spirit.

Invite a smile to your face. When you are completely at peace, let your loved one know you are present and available. Say "I am here for you, beloved. I am grateful you are here!"

Continue to focus on staying present and listening for any sound or voice that may place a word, phrase or song in your mind.

Listen. Note whatever happens, whatever impression or thought pops into your mind. Write down everything you feel and hear in your journal.

Practice in this way for 20-30 minutes.

Change is always difficult, but dedicating yourself to speaking with your loved one in spirit brings its own rewards even if your initial attempts are challenging.

What can you expect?

1. As your awareness grows, you will begin to understand the deeper messages behind the synchronicities you observe.
2. Your loved one in heaven is aware that you are trying to reach them and that's exciting! Your loved one will work with angels and guides for help in making this happen in a way that is right for both of you.
3. Through your efforts to connect, your spiritual path becomes illuminated. You will see where your steps are taking you and recognize the destination.
4. You will become closer to the divine source and begin to accept the divinity in your own soul.
5. Finally, you will find ways to have your loved one with you on your earth journey. That person wants to connect with you and be a voice in your life.

Congratulations! You've reached the end of our 21-day journey together.

Thank you for your exploration and for your determination to converse with those who have transitioned to heaven.

Works Cited

1. Expect an Answer (Anonymous, 2019)
2. Byrne, Lorna. *Angels in My Hair.* Three Rivers Press, Random House, Inc., 2008
3. Crowley Fathers. *The Rule of the Society of St. John the Evangelist.* (p.82) Rowman & Littlefield Publishers, Inc., 1997
4. Farrington, Debra K. *Hearing with Heart.* (p.86) Jossey-Bass, 2003
5. Kessler, David. *Finding Meaning, the Sixth Sense of Grief.* (p.78) Simon& Schuster, Inc., 2019
6. Noe, Karen. *The Rainbow Follows the Storm.* (p.90) Blue Dolphin Publishing, Inc., 2005
7. Triffet, Carrie. *The Enlightenment Project.* Gentle Joyous Industries, 2011
8. Tolle, Eckhart. *Stillness Speaks.* (p.71) Namaste Publishing, 2003
9. Tozer, A.W. *The Pursuit of God.* Millennium Publications, 2014
10. Williamson, Marianne. *Teaching the Teachers video course, Day 4.* Commune, 2019

Additional Study

Audio Track

Mindfulness class available on InSight Timer cell phone application:

Deepen Your Meditation Practice with Poetry by Hugh Byrne

Books

<u>Through the Eyes of Another</u> *by Karen Noe,* focuses on current life review and letter writing

<u>We Consciousness</u> *by Karen Noe,* details approach to achieving inner peace

<u>Silence: The Power of Quiet in a World Full of Noise -</u> how to find and maintain inner peace *by Thich Nhat Hanh*

Organization

Helping Parents Heal is a non-profit organization dedicated to assisting bereaved parents to become Shining Light Parents by providing support and resources to aid in the healing process. This organization allows the open discussion of spiritual experiences and evidence for the afterlife.

https://www.helpingparentsheal.org/

Made in the USA
Coppell, TX
03 October 2020